P9-DME-975

HIDE AND SEEK

FIRST WORDS

DK
DK Publishing

Notes for parents

Hide-and-seek First Words is a great picture book for you and your child to share. Filled with wonderful objects to find and talk about, this book will help your child build vocabulary, learn colors, practice counting, and develop observation skills.

To get the most out of this book

- Talk about all the things you see on each page. Point to the objects, say their names, then hunt for each one together. As children become familiar with the book, they will be able to name and find the objects themselves.

- Encourage your child to describe the different things. What color or shape are they? What are they made of? Which one is your child's favorite? Do you have something similar at home?

- Read the rhymes and let your child say them with you. Then help your child find the objects in the rhymes.

- Once your child knows letter sounds, you can play traditional "I spy." Ask your child to find an object on the page that begins with a certain letter.

DK

LONDON, NEW YORK,
MELBOURNE, MUNICH, AND DELHI

Written by Dawn Sirett
Designed by Rachael Parfitt and Victoria Palastanga
Special Photography by Dave King
Illustrations by Rachael Parfitt and Victoria Palastanga
U.S. Editor Jennifer Quasha
Production Controller Louise Kelly
Production Editor Andy Hilliard

First published in the United States in 2010
by DK Publishing
375 Hudson Street
New York, New York 10014

10 11 12 13 14 10 9 8 7 6 5 4 3 2 1
177754—06/10

Copyright © 2010 Dorling Kindersley Limited

All rights reserved under International and Pan-American Copyright
Conventions. No part of this publication may be reproduced, stored in a retrieval
system, or transmitted in any form or by any means, electronic, mechanical,
photocopying, recording, or otherwise, without the prior written permission of the
copyright owner. Published in Great Britain by Dorling Kindersley Limited.

DK books are available at special discounts when purchased in bulk for sales
promotions, premiums, fund-raising, or educational use. For details, contact:
DK Publishing Special Markets
375 Hudson Street
New York, New York 10014
SpecialSales@dk.com

A catalog record for this book is available from the Library of Congress.

ISBN 978-0-7566-6300-1

Printed and bound in China by Leo Paper Products

Discover more at
www.dk.com

a dump truck

a pair of sparkly shoes

a spinning top

a plastic ring

a motorcycle

a watering can

Contents

a shirt

a clock

a wool hat

a xylophone

Boo!

This is Buzzy Bee. He is on every page of this book! Can you find him?

Toy shelf

Let's find...

a duck

a teddy bear

a ball

a train

a doll

a tower of stacking cups

a camera

a spinning top

a jar of marbles

a penguin

an elephant

a hobby horse

a caterpillar

a snail

a drum

a crocodile

a cat

a rocket

3 wooden people

2 fire trucks

a fire fighter

a robot

a dinosaur

I spy a red race car.
If you see it, you're a star!

4

5

Clothes
Let's find...

pajamas

a T-shirt

a pair of underpants

a bathrobe

a pair of slippers

2 sweaters

a pair of overalls

a pair of sneakers

a dress

a watch

a scarf

a skirt

a jacket

a pair of pants

a pair of socks

a pair of sparkly shoes

2 white buttons

a hairbrush

a comb

a belt

a raincoat

an umbrella

Choose your
favorite thing to wear,
then find a little
teddy bear.

Animals

Let's find...

an elephant

a spider

a giraffe

a horse

a mouse

a dinosaur

a kangaroo and joey

a dog

a lion

a hippo

2 snakes

3 ducks

a zebra

a pig

a crocodile

a cow

a frog

a rabbit

8

Which creature has been caught for lunch? Can he escape before he's munched?

In the garden

Let's find...

a butterfly

4 bulbs

a trowel

3 snails

a spider

a striped plant pot

a yellow watering can

a ball of string

a dragonfly

3 ladybugs

a frog

a fork

a pair of gloves

2 sunflowers

a bird

a birdhouse

a rake

a pair of boots

Can you see a tiny man with his own small watering can?

Colors

Let's find...

a green paintbrush

a red lipstick

a purple comb

a man in blue

a yellow bus

an orange flower

a green leaf

a green bug

a red mouse

a purple butterfly

12

a yellow chick

an orange bracelet

1 green circle

3 orange triangles

2 blue rectangles

If you can find a tiny bed, you'll see a teeny sleepyhead!

a blue dinosaur

a red strawberry

3 yellow squares

7 purple stars

1 red heart

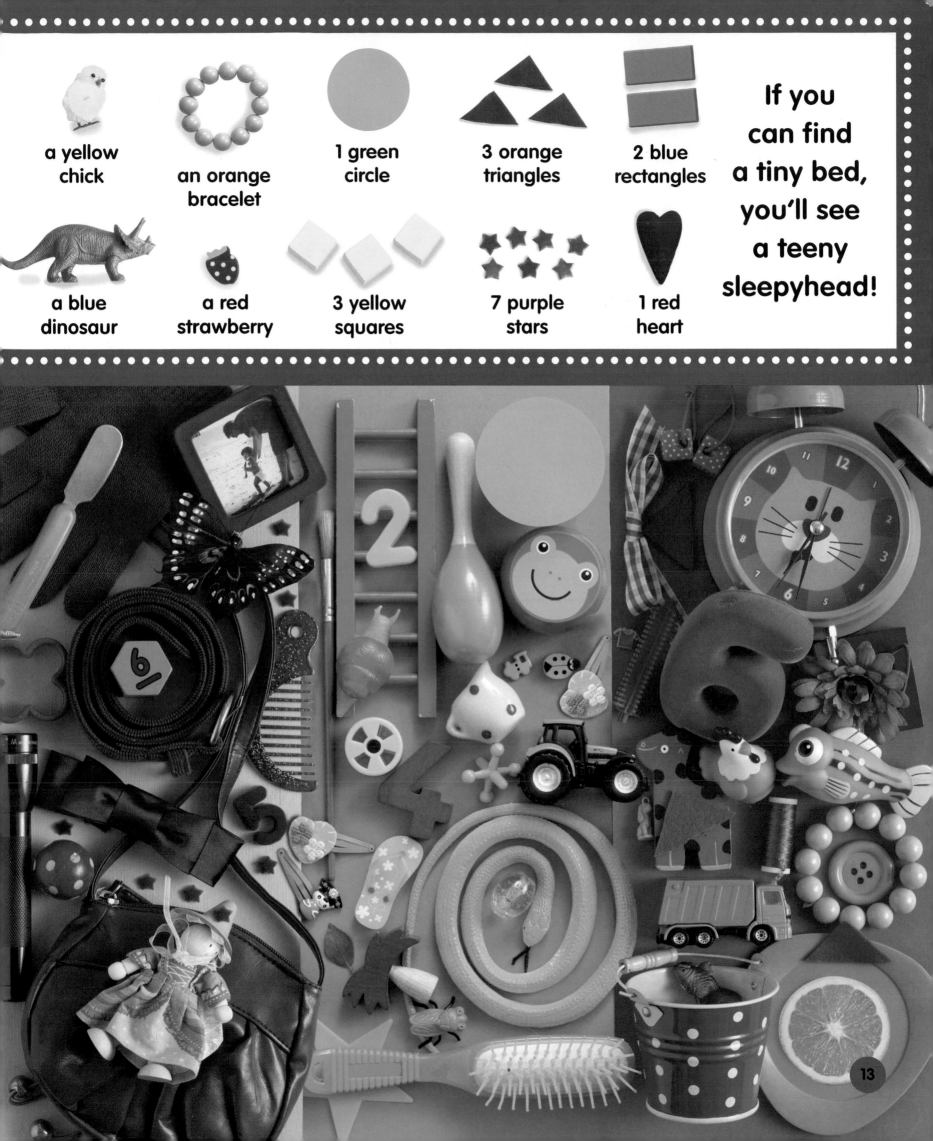

13

Play school

Let's find...

a painting

a pair of scissors

a pencil case

a frog calculator

a jump rope

3 crayons

a ruler

a pencil sharpener

a stapler

a soccer ball eraser

3 tubes of glitter

a blackboard

a pair of glasses

a pen

a paint palette

3 paintbrushes

a piece of chalk

a magnet

3 red stars

a glue pen

a magnifying glass

a clock

4 bottles of paint

2 toy children

a notebook

a globe

I spy a little kitty cat
and a girl with an orange hat.

Dots and stripes

Let's find...

a present

a dog rattle

5 red-and-white mushrooms

a caterpillar

a leopard

a domino

a fish

a red-and-white bow

a rainbow purse

a notebook

4 pencils

a pair of mittens

a rainbow

a tiger

a plate

a cup and saucer

a wool hat

a dice

a teddy bear

Meow! Meow! Who said that? Do you see the happy striped cat?

At the beach

Let's find...

a sand castle

2 sailboats

a kite

a pair of
sandals

a cap

a pair of
binoculars

a swimsuit

a bucket

a dolphin

a flag

a bathing
suit

a shovel

4 pebbles

a pair of
sunglasses

a pair of
flippers

an ice cream
cone

a plastic
ring

a snorkel

a mask

a pinwheel

Somewhere
at the beach I spy
a scaly turtle creeping by.

In the kitchen

Let's find...

a mug

a colander

a grater

a kettle

a vase of flowers

3 spoons

a clock

a box of tissues

a bowl of fruit

a framed photo

a blue pitcher

a spatula

a kitchen towel

a pair of tongs

3 bowls

a vegetable peeler

a casserole dish

a scrub brush

3 hooks

a blue serving spoon

a sieve

2 keys

a tray

a pot

I spy two big eyes and a mouth so wide
you can fit a kitchen sponge inside!

Things that go

Let's find...

a motorcycle

2 blue-and-red planes

a hot-air balloon

a sailboat

2 orange-and-green race cars

3 red cars

an off-road vehicle

a scooter

a tractor with loader

a helicopter

a truck

a garbage truck

a bus

a fire truck

Look at all
the things to drive,
then find the number 55.

Play cooking

Let's find...

a jar
of jam

a blue
mixing bowl

3 cookies

a rolling pin

a heart
cookie cutter

4 pink cupcakes

4 pasta shapes

a jelly
mold

a spoon

a knife

an oven
mitt

a fork

4 empty cupcake molds

a wooden
spoon

some raisins

a whisk

a scale

a cake stand

24

Find three candles
on three cupcakes,
and two hearts
cut out to bake.

Busy builders

Let's find...

7 striped cones

a dump truck

a wheel loader

a backhoe loader

2 jackhammers

a bulldozer

One busy builder
has a call from home.
Can you see the
small cell phone?

a paver

a builder with
a purple hat

a roller

4 tool boxes

a wheelbarrow

a concrete
mixer truck

a hammer

a pick axe

an excavator

a tower

a ladder

a saw

a bucket

27

Black and white

Let's find...

a magician's wand

a bow tie

a rabbit

a pair of glasses

2 wheels

a polar bear

a pair of shoes

a piano

2 ghosts

a panda

Find a mouse playing a tune, and a couple marrying soon!

28

a skeleton

a blackbird

an egg

3 bats

a plastic hat

a cauldron

8 dominoes

a monkey

3 soccer balls

3 black cats

a Dalmatian

Bathtime

Let's find...

a fishing net

a butterfly soap

a bottle of shampoo

a yellow towel

a crab

a soap dish

a mermaid

a bottle of bubble bath

a starfish

a nailbrush

a seal

a sea horse

3 toothbrushes

a big yellow duck

a blue-and-yellow diver

2 green boats

Look here, there ... ...and everywhere for six bubbles in the air.

Dollhouse

Let's find...

a bath

2 pink chairs

a bike

a lamp

a toaster

a bunk bed

a rabbit hutch

a green bureau

a sofa

a shower

a table

Dad, Mom, 2 children, and the baby

a kitchen sink

a highchair

a pot

a train

a stove and oven

a wagon

a television

a computer

a rocking horse

a bed

a toilet

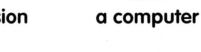
2 big windows

a crib

I spy with my little eye
a dog and a rabbit, and a cat up high.

On the farm

Let's find...

4 ducklings

2 cows

2 sheep

a tractor

a donkey

2 farmers

4 chickens

a rooster

4 horses

2 milk cans

a basket of vegetables

a dog

a kennel

a tire

a pitchfork

a turkey

a kid

a goat

a pig

2 piglets

a pigsty

a green ladder

Somewhere hiding
for you to seek,
are three farm mice.
Squeak, squeak, squeak!

Musical things
Let's find...

a recorder

a trumpet

2 cymbals

2 maracas

a triangle

a xylophone

8 gold bells

a drum

2 harmonicas

a bongo drum

an accordion

a tambourine

3 kazoos

an electric guitar

a keyboard

Spy a
frog that goes
click click. You
can do it—you're
so quick!

Story time

Let's find...

the Queen

the King

a dragon

a witch's cat

a glass slipper

2 ballerinas

a horse and carriage

a tower

a witch

2 princesses

a fairy
godmother

the moon

2 fairies

3 fish

a lion

a prince

a mermaid

a superhero

a wizard

Spy two magic wands,
then here's what you do...

...make a special wish
that you'd like
to come true!

Treasure hunt

Let's find...

a treasure chest

a key

a parrot

a crown

a pirate ship

a gold buckle

a green heart jewel

6 wooden pirates

a charm bracelet

a monkey

10 gold coins

a brooch

a fob watch

a treasure map

a sword

a compass

a book

a quill pen

a starfish

a telescope

a ruby ring

a scroll

a pirate's hat

More sparkly jewels are buried in the ground. I spy the "X" where they can be found!

Numbers

Let's find the number...

 zero

 one

 two

 three

four

 five

 six

seven

eight

nine

ten

 eleven

 twelve

thirteen

 fourteen

fifteen

sixteen

seventeen

 eighteen

nineteen

twenty

fifty

 one hundred

Now let's count...

 2 rainbows

2 green stars

 3 yellow planets

 5 candles

How old are you? Five, four, or three?
And where's that number? Do you see?

Christmas

Let's find...

a penguin

a Christmas tree

a tiny Santa

an owl

a red spotted ornament

a dancing Santa

2 candy canes

a teddy bear

a sled and rider

a spotted star

an angel

2 snowmen

3 blue candies

2 pinecones

a reindeer

a stocking

5 green ornaments

44

Find a letter. Who's it to?
What would you write
if it was from you?

45

More to find!

You'll find all these things if you go back and look at the big, busy pictures in this hide-and-seek book!

a lemon

a mirror

a red
polka-dotted kettle

a police car

a saxophone

3 skateboards

a yellow spatula

a cake knife

an orange
cat clock

a bookshelf

a yellow
concrete mixer

a car transporter

2 cowboys

2 oranges

an orange
slice

a pair
of tights

a green
tractor

a tomato

a bag of flour

a pirate skull
eye patch

"Bye-bye!" says Buzzy Bee. "How many times did you find me?"

Bye-bye!

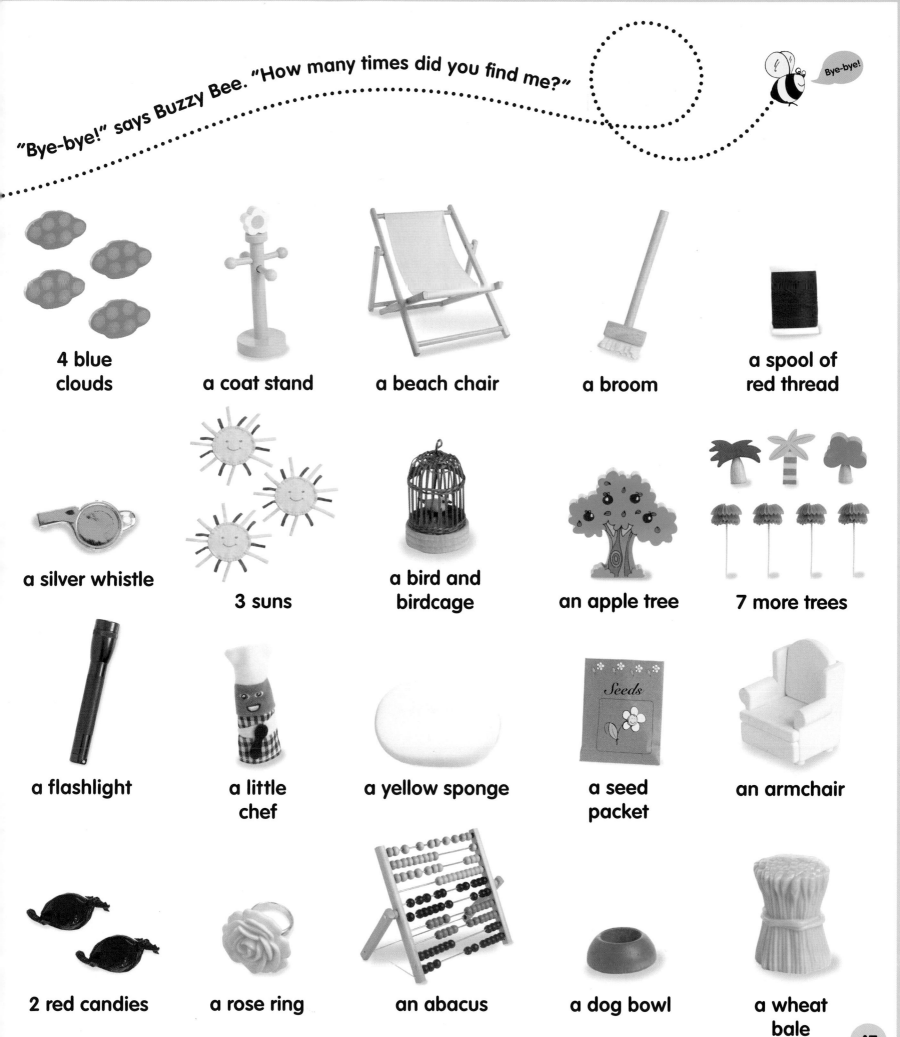

4 blue clouds

a coat stand

a beach chair

a broom

a spool of red thread

a silver whistle

3 suns

a bird and birdcage

an apple tree

7 more trees

a flashlight

a little chef

a yellow sponge

a seed packet

an armchair

2 red candies

a rose ring

an abacus

a dog bowl

a wheat bale

Index of words we've found!

abacus 47
accordion 36
angel 44
apple tree 47
armchair 47

baby 12, 13, 32
backhoe loader 26
ball 4
ballerinas 38
bath 32
bathing suit 18
bathrobe 6
bats 29
beach chair 47
bed 12, 13, 32
bells 36
belt 6
bike 32
binoculars 18
birdcage 47
birdhouse 10
birds 10, 29, 40, 47
blackboard 14
boats 18, 22, 30
bongo drum 36
book 40
bookshelf 46
boots 10
bow 16
bow tie 28
bowls 20, 24, 47
bracelet 13, 40
bride and groom 29
brooch 40
broom 47
bubble bath 30
bubbles 30, 31
bucket 18, 27
buckle 40
bug 12
builder 26, 27
bulbs 10
bulldozer 26
bunk bed 32
bureau 32
bus 12, 22
butterfly 10, 12, 30
buttons 6

Cake knife 46
cake stand 24
calculator 14
camera 4
candies 44, 47
candles 25, 42
candy canes 44
cap 18
car transporter 46
cars 4, 5, 22, 46
casserole dish 20
castanet 37
caterpillar 4, 16
cats 4, 14, 15, 16, 17,
    29, 33, 46
cauldron 29

cell phone 26, 27
chairs 32, 47
chalk 14
chef 47
chick 13
children 14, 32
Christmas tree 44
circle 13
clock 3, 14, 20, 46
clouds 47
coat stand 47
coins 40
colander 20
comb 6, 12
compass 40
computer 32
concrete mixer 46
concrete mixer truck 27
cones 26
cookie cutter 24
cookies 24
couple 28, 29
cowboys 46
cows 8, 34
crab 30
crayons 14
crib 32
crocodile 4, 8
crown 40
cup and saucer 16
cupcakes 24, 25
cymbals 36

dad 32
Dalmatian 29
dice 17
dinosaur 4, 8, 13
diver 30
dog 8, 16, 33, 35
dog bowl 47
doll 4
dolphin 18
dominoes 16, 29
donkey 34
dragon 38
dragonfly 10
dress 6
drums 4, 36
ducks 4, 8, 30
ducklings 34
dump truck 3, 26

egg 29
electric guitar 36
elephant 4, 8
eraser 14
excavator 27
eye patch 46
eyes 20, 21

fairies 39
fairy godmother 39
farmers 34
fire fighter 4
fire trucks 4, 22
fish 9, 16, 39
fishing net 30
flag 18
flashlight 47
flippers 18

flour 46
flowers 12, 20
fob watch 40
fork 10, 24
framed photo 20
frog 8, 10, 14, 21, 37
fruit 13, 20, 46, 47

garbage truck 22
ghosts 28
giraffe 8
girl 14, 15
glass slipper 38
glasses 14, 28
glitter 14
globe 14
gloves 10
glue pen 14
goat 35
grater 20
guitar 36

hairbrush 6
hammer 27
harmonicas 36
hat 3, 14, 15, 17, 18, 29, 40
hearts 13, 24, 25, 40
helicopter 22
hens 34
highchair 32
hippo 8
hobby horse 4
hooks 20
horse and carriage 38
horses 4, 8, 32, 35, 38
hot-air balloon 22

ice cream cone 18

jacket 6
jackhammers 26
jam 24
jelly mold 24
jewels 40
joey 8
jump rope 14

kangaroo 8
kazoos 36
kennel 35
kettle 20, 46
keyboard 36
keys 20, 40
kid 35
king 38
kitchen towel 20
kite 18
knife 24, 46

ladder 27, 35
ladybugs 10
lamp 32
leaf 12
lemon 46
leopard 16
letter 44, 45
lion 8, 39
lipstick 12

magic wands 38, 39
magician's wand 20
magnet 14
magnifying glass 14

man 11, 12
maracas 36
marbles 4
mask 18
mermaid 30, 39
mice 8, 12, 28, 29, 34, 35
milk cans 35
mirror 46
mittens 17
mom 32
monkey 29, 40
moon 39
motorcycle 3, 22
mouth 20, 21
mug 20
mushrooms 16

nailbrush 30
notebook 14, 17
numbers 22, 23, 42, 43

Off-road vehicle 22
orange slice 46
oranges 46
ornaments 44
oven 32
oven mitt 24
overalls 6
owl 44

paint 14
paint palette 14
paintbrushes 12, 14
painting 14
pajamas 6
panda 28
pants 6
parrot 40
pasta shapes 24
paver 27
pebbles 18
pen 14, 40
pencil case 14
pencil sharpener 14
pencils 14, 17
penguin 4, 44
people 4
photo 20
piano 28
pick axe 27
pig 8, 35
piglets 35
pigsty 35
pinecones 44
pinwheel 18
pirate ship 40
pirate skull 46
pirate's hat 40
pirates 40
pitcher 20
pitchfork 35
planes 22
planets 42
plant pot 10
plastic ring 3, 18
plate 17
polar bear 28
pot 20, 32
present 16
prince 39

princesses 39
purse 17

queen 38
quill pen 40

rabbit 8, 28, 33
rabbit hutch 32
rainbows 17, 42
raincoat 6
raisins 24
rake 10
rattle 16
recorder 36
rectangles 13
reindeer 44
rider 44
ring 3, 18, 40, 47
robot 4
rocket 4
rocking horse 32
roller 27
rolling pin 24
rooster 34
ruler 14

Sand castle 18
sandals 18
Santa 44
saw 27
saxophone 46
scale 24
scarf 6
scissors 14
scooter 22
scroll 40
scrub brush 20
sea horse 30
seal 30
seed packet 47
serving spoon 20
shampoo 30
sheep 34
shirt 3
shoes 3, 6, 18, 28, 38
shovel 18
shower 32
sieve 20
sink 32
skateboards 46
skeleton 29
skirt 6
sled 44
sleepyhead 12, 13
slippers 6
snails 4, 10
snakes 8
sneakers 6
snorkel 18
snowmen 44
soap 30
soap dish 30
soccer balls 14, 29
socks 6
sofa 32
spatula 20, 46
spiders 8, 10
spinning top 3, 4
sponge 20, 21, 47
spool of thread 47
spoons 20, 24

squares 13
stacking cups 4
stapler 14
starfish 30, 40
stars 13, 14, 42, 44
stocking 44
stove 32
strawberry 13
string 10
sunflowers 10
sunglasses 18
suns 47
superhero 39
sweaters 6
swimsuit 18
sword 40

table 32
tambourine 36
teddy bear 4, 6, 7, 17, 44
telescope 40
television 32
tiger 17
tights 46
tire 35
tissues 20
toaster 32
toilet 32
tomato 46
tongs 20
tool boxes 27
toothbrushes 30
towel 30
tower 4, 27, 38
tractor 22, 34, 46
train 4, 32
tray 20
treasure chest 40
treasure map 40
trees 44, 47
triangles 13, 36
trowel 10
trucks 3, 4, 22, 26, 27
trumpet 36
T-shirt 6
turkey 35
turtle 18, 19

Umbrella 6
underpants 6

Vegetable peeler 20
vegetables 35

Wagon 32
watch 6, 40
watering can 3, 10, 11
wheat bale 47
wheel loader 26
wheelbarrow 27
wheels 28
whisk 24
whistle 47
windows 32
witch 39
witch's cat 38
wizard 38
wooden spoon 24

Xylophone 3, 36

Zebra 8